"This remarkable handbook offers more than simply exercises to heighten sexual intensity and satisfaction for couples. It provides a focus that deepens emotional, mental, *and* physical connections."

— Sol S. Rosenberg, Ph.D.
Past President, American Academy of Psychotherapists
Past President, Illinois Psychological Association

"This insightful workbook offers couples the potential for growth and renewal. Dr. Shaw's focus on respectful authenticity and self-responsibility in intimate partnerships also makes this a useful adjunct to couples therapy."

— Elaine L. Levin, Ph.D., ABPP
Psychologist

"Dr. Shaw is not only knowledgeable about human sexuality and how to make it work, she comes with a kind heart, an honest mind, and twinkling eyes. She has given us a handbook which I know from my own experience is a powerful medium whether used in privacy or with professional guidance."

— Leonard Schwartzburd, Ph.D.
CEO and Director of Psychological Services
The Clinical Institute of Behavioral Medicine
Berkeley, California

"...these creative exercises encourage couples to stay *in* relationship while each partner develops the courage to be deeply sexual with the other. We recommend it without reservation to anyone who wants to improve intimacy..."

— Frances Nagata, R.N., M.S.N., Sex and Marital Therapist
— Rev. Dr. William M. Nagata, Chaplain (Col.)
U.S. Army (Ret.)

"...I would encourage any couple who cares about each other to use this handbook as a tool to increase sexual enjoyment and ability to communicate more effectively and willingly about *anything!*"

— Beverly Kievman Copen
   Author of *For Better or for Worse: A couples guide to dealing with chronic Illness*

"These verbal exercises demystify a highly personal topic and point the way toward increasing sexual energy, especially for people in long-term relationships. I applaud this work."

— Kitty La Perriere, Ph.D.
   Past President, American Family Therapy Association

"Journey Toward Intimacy *excellently* compliments the work of marriage and family counselors. It is the best example of 'homework' in the field of sex therapy."

— Sol Gordon, Ph.D.
   Professor Emeritus of Child and Family Studies, Syracuse University
   Author of *Why Love Is Not Enough*

"My mother's sincerity, insightfulness, and genuine desire to help others enrich their lives is a constant source of inspiration for me."

— Rabbi Joseph L. Shaw
   Jerusalem, Israel

Journey
Toward Intimacy
A Handbook for Couples

Jeanne Shaw, Ph.D.

Revised Edition

Couples Enrichment Institute
P. O. Box 420114
Atlanta, Georgia 30342-0114

Journey Toward Intimacy
A Handbook for Couples

Jeanne Shaw, Ph.D.

Published by:

The Couples Enrichment Institute
P.O. Box 420114
Atlanta, GA 30342-0114

Copyright ® 1998 by Jeanne Shaw, Ph.D.

Printed in the United States of America

ISBN 1-891257-04-8 (pbk) Revised Edition

Library of Congress Catalogue Card Number 98-92432

CONTENTS

Warning - Disclaimer

This book is meant to provide information to couples on the subject matter covered. It is sold with the understanding that the publisher and the author are not engaged in rendering professional services through this book. Although the book may be used effectively in conjunction with therapy, it does not take the place of therapy. If counseling is required, a *licensed* mental health professional should be contracted.

It is not within the scope of this handbook to provide *complete* information on the topic but rather to stir you to acquire further information. You are urged to read available material about sexual relationships and fit the information to your own circumstances. For a brief list of references, please see Suggested Readings in the Appendix.

Every effort has been made to make this handbook concise and accurate. However, there may be mistakes, both typographical and in content. Further, standards for couples' sexual behavior change with social change; thus, some concepts basic to this handbook may shift over time.

The purpose of this handbook is to educate and inspire you toward fulfilling your human potential. The author and the Couples Enrichment Institute has neither liability nor responsibility to any person or couple with respect to any loss or damage caused or alleged to have been caused, directly or indirectly, by the use of information contained herein.

If you do not wish to be bound by the above, you may return this book unused to the publisher for a full refund.

Welcome to the Handbook!

Journey Toward Intimacy is for couples who want a lasting, intimate, juicy sexual relationship as well as for couples who are bored or unfulfilled. You will be introduced to new perspectives of being sexually intimate with your partner and invited to risk being erotic without the help of fantasies, videos, sex toys, or genital techniques. The handbook offers an experience like the Retreat for Couples workshop (for which it was designed) without the expense or support of a weekend workshop. At home, you can plan each exercise at your own pace, daily, weekly, monthly.

More than twenty years of searching for what is *right* with hundreds of couples who enjoy exclusive, sexually active, lifelong relationships reveals surprisingly simple, if discomforting, answers. Their collective wisdom is here in the form of written and verbal exercises.

Although this is not a techniques manual on sexual arousal or desire, your partner may respond when you touch a heart with love. These exercises can give new perspectives, support, and basic experiences for enriching sexual intimacy. You will soon discover how integrity acts as an aphrodisiac.

In the first two years of a new relationship, partners are usually lusty and loving while putting forward their most attractive traits. Under the influence of potent chemistry, lovers will not be convinced of the temporary nature of their initial lust. Fortunately, lust does not last, for if it did, the flow of emotionally and erotically intimate growth would wane. Here is a radical thought: Lackluster sex is a signal of fertile possibilities. Your natural emotional and sexual energy will move you toward your potential for full sexual, intimate expression until something interferes. You remove the interference by further developing your integrity, maturity, and good sense of humor. *Erotic* intimate sex with a life partner depends on it.

These exercises are reported to be rewarding, eye-opening, and a bit nerve-racking for couples not in the habit of talking about their real experience. Designed to lead you into new emotional and mindful territory, the exercises expose you to self-recognition and ask you to claim sexual authorship of yourself in your own committed relationship.

There is no wrong way to approach the exercises: joyfully, sadly, aggressively, timidly, skillfully, awkwardly, hopefully, skeptically. All lead to self-knowledge.

Suggestions:

1. Read the suggestions at the beginning of each exercise and do the exercise.

2. Make an appointment with your partner to compare and discuss responses, especially tough ones.

3. Don't explode, don't cave in, and don't leave. Just quiet yourself.

4. The discussion following each exercise is where you shift your thinking. Although you can skip around, doing the exercises in sequence may soften your journey.

5. After each discussion, talk about how it was for you to discuss that particular topic. *This is vital.*

Good Journey!

Purposes

1. Observe how your own beliefs, attitudes, and development affect your sexual energy.

2. Learn why knowing yourself better leads to sexual enthusiasm with your life partner.

3. Recognize which thoughts, feelings, and behaviors enhance or block sexual energy or expression with your partner.

4. Explore the significance of anxiety-reducing behaviors (safe, familiar, comfortable, friendly, cozy) and anxiety-producing behaviors (risky, unfamiliar, uncomfortable, erotic).

5. Emphasize intimacy and erotic feelings during sex instead of fantasy or technique.

6. Learn how partner-validation builds good-will and how self-validation builds sexual maturity.

7. Explore your own style for self-development and sexual intimacy in relationship.

Write or consider your responses to the following statements and then share them with your partner.

My wish for *myself* in completing this handbook:

My wish for my *partner* in completing this handbook:

My hope for our *relationship*:

I am willing to struggle with myself while I am with my partner and talk about issues I find very hard to think about, let alone discuss:

☐ Yes   ☐ No

Other comments:

Sexual Attitudes

The first exercise surveys your sexual attitudes. Attitudes can support or weaken your connection and desire for each other. They are rarely neutral. As people mature, attitudes change. Partners can stay in touch by noting obvious and subtle changes, together and independently.

Your attitudes have meaning. When you are willing to understand their meaning to you and to your partner, you can connect purposefully instead of accidentally, resentfully, or not at all. You create options for contact when you are willing to understand how your thinking affects your behavior. Wanting to know yourself and enhance sexual behavior with your partner is a developmental task. Developing yourself in relationship should be a deeply satisfying, if awkward, experience. Awkwardness comes with knowing how some of your attitudes cheat you and reward you (with shame or joy for your sexuality, for example).

To develop yourself in relationship, you have to be present. Presence fosters emotional intimacy and sexual options and is a result of self-awareness. Presence may also increase anxiety. Although emotional presence is a choice, the capacity for it is developed with self-awareness and tolerance for the uneasiness of being deeply connected.

Thus, self-awareness helps you recognize your attitudes and how they affect your sex life. Self-awareness helps you respond without overreacting or withholding the truth of your experience. You gain integrity when good will and self-respect prevail over your anxiety and self-defeating attitudes. But first you must know what they are.

Suggestions:

1. Fill out the "Sexual Attitude Survey" quickly and spontaneously. There are no wrong answers.

2. Make enough time to compare responses. Each response will have a unique meaning to each of you.

3. Although agreement and difference are both vital to sexual aliveness, you learn more from differences.

4. With each useful obstacle, either partner can inquire, "What does this mean?" "What is my part?" And with each useless obstacle, "Do I need to keep it?"

5. Don't explode, don't cave in, and don't leave. Just quiet yourself. Continue talking or agree to continue later, and honor your agreements.

6. Afterwards, talk abcut what it was like to discuss your sexual attitudes.

Sexual Attitude Survey

Indicate whether you **A**gree or **D**isagree:

( )   1. Sex is perfect, nothing needs to change (skip this question if you fell in love recently).

( )   2. By now, my partner should be sensitive enough to know what turns me on without my saying so.

( )   3. Sex should be easy and spontaneous.

( )   4. I surprise myself with new ways to make love.

( )   5. I tell my partner what pleasures me sexually and what does not arouse me.

( )   6. At times in my life I have had sex when I did not really want to, just to please my partner.

( )   7. I enhance my own arousal by having a sexual fantasy while having sex with my partner.

( )   8. I wish I could ignore my partner's desire for sex, but s/he tries so hard to please, I feel guilty.

( )   9. I could behave more erotically if I thought my partner could handle how intensely sexual I feel.

( ) 10. I can tell when my partner is not really with me during sex, when s/he is having a fantasy.

( ) 11. I can enjoy self-stimulation or having my genitals stroked/kissed instead of penis-in-vagina sex.

( ) 12. Sex for me is often monotonous or boring.

( ) 13. I want to give my partner what she or he wants but I do not actually know how.

( ) 14. Something is missing sexually that I cannot name.

( ) 15. I am confident in my ability to arouse my partner.

( ) 16. I do not say how I feel when I think my partner will get upset.

( ) 17. I would like to explore being uninhibited.

( ) 18. I have faked orgasms.

( ) 19. My partner should agree to sex when I want it.

( ) 20. To enjoy sex, I must feel emotionally connected.

( ) 21. To feel emotionally connected, first I need sex.

( ) 22. I am going to have a hard time telling my partner something negative that will upset him/her.

Common Misinformed Beliefs About Sex

The next exercise offers twenty common misinformed beliefs about sex. Any one of them can sabotage enjoyment of your sexuality. You may believe some of them are true, depending on how, when, and where you grew up. Most partners have differences in beliefs. Exploring these differences permits you to know more about yourself and how you manage differences in values and attitudes.

Almost every man and woman in our culture is taught, unintentionally, to undermine their natural sexuality. Children are shamed for behaving in certain ways, and erroneous beliefs become seen as truths. You can repair this by recognizing and restructuring the errors in your sexual beliefs. You can learn most effectively with gentle discussion. Active listening (not feeling attacked, blamed, or criticized) will help you hear your partner and inhibit your inner critic.

You may profit from reading a good sex education book together. Your partner will tell you if you would benefit. Clergy, libraries, SIECUS, AASECT (see Community Resources, p. 105), internet access, and most bookstores can help you locate good references. Sexual education is neither pornography nor erotica. Its intent is not to arouse you, but to provide accurate information about the physical and emotional skills necessary to a satisfying sexual relationship.

Suggestions for Reading Common Misinformed Beliefs

1. Mark each belief in the first list as true or false, according to your own belief.

2. Make enough time with your partner to compare and discuss responses.

3. If you have major disagreements and one of you believes your idea is true, decide what it means in your relationship that you hold different beliefs (e.g., how disagreement affects your thinking and your sexual pilot light.)

4. Don't explode, don't cave in, and don't leave. Just quiet yourself.

5. After you complete the exercise, talk about how it was for you to discuss this topic. Was it difficult, easy, stirring, boring, enjoyable, insightful, risky?

Common Misinformed Beliefs about Sex

☐ When she is wet, she is ready.

☐ Unless he has an erection, he does not love her.

☐ Foreplay is for the woman, intercourse for the man.

☐ If you love each other and communicate well, good sex will follow.

☐ Sexual problems mean something is wrong in the relationship.

☐ Casual sex is more exciting than intimate sex.

☐ In a good sexual relationship, you have a fulfilling experience every time.

☐ After age 25 your sex drive decreases and stops altogether by age 65.

☐ It is the man's role to initiate sex.

☐ If either partner is aroused, intercourse must follow.

☐ Having "G" spot and multiple orgasms means a woman is sexually liberated.

☐ Menopause decreases sexual desire.

☐ When you lose sexual desire for your partner, the best remedy is to find another partner.

- [ ] A man with a big penis is a highly skilled lover.

- [ ] Large-breasted women are more easily aroused than small-breasted women.

- [ ] Married people do not masturbate.

- [ ] Once you learn the sexual ropes, you are set for life.

- [ ] The best sex is spontaneous and unplanned.

- [ ] Penis-in-vagina is the only sex that really counts.

- [ ] The best sex with your partner is to close your eyes and have an orgasm via sexual fantasy.

- [ ] If I do not arouse her/him, I am not performing as I should.

- [ ] Successful sex means I have (and give my partner) an orgasm every time.

Commentary on Misinformed Beliefs

WHEN SHE IS WET, SHE IS READY. Not necessarily. Some women get wet before they have an awareness of arousal, and others feel intensely aroused without ever lubricating.

UNLESS HE HAS AN ERECTION, HE DOES NOT LOVE HER. Erections are an indication of physiological arousal, not a measure of love, i.e., the plumbing is intact. Men get (and lose) erections for a variety of reasons, such as contributing to the gene pool, expressing love and lust, and relief from pressure, anxiety, and stress. He can also get an erection without loving her.

FOREPLAY IS FOR THE WOMAN, INTERCOURSE IS FOR THE MAN. Foreplay communicates what will happen next and how it will happen. To portray women as romantic and men as averse to intense arousal is a disservice to both. Many, if not most, men love foreplay, and many women want the feel of penis-in-vagina.

IF YOU LOVE EACH OTHER AND COMMUNICATE WELL, GOOD SEX WILL FOLLOW. Not so for more than half the loving, skillfully communicating couples in America. Communication is necessary but not sufficient for erotic sex. You build good sex with self-support, self-soothing, self-validation, integrity, emotional intimacy, and physical skill.

SEXUAL PROBLEMS MEAN SOMETHING IS WRONG IN THE RELATIONSHIP. A relationship ripe for growth may use a sexual problem as a signal, instead of words. Or, there could be a physical problem. The purpose is ultimately to elicit attention to a physical or relational signal. Relationships without problems go

19

stale. And you can have good sex even though something is wrong in the relationship.

CASUAL SEX IS MORE EXCITING THAN INTIMATE SEX. Nothing is more exciting or potentially nerve-racking than intimate, erotic sex between long-term partners. Casual sex can be novel at first, but a purely genital focus becomes monotonous when that is all there is.

IN A GOOD SEXUAL RELATIONSHIP YOU HAVE A FUL-FILLING EXPERIENCE EVERY TIME. Not hardly. Sex and everything else in life has cycles. Sex will be tepid, mind-blowing, monotonous, delightful, adequate, and stunning, depending on mental, physical, emotional, environmental, relational, and other variables.

AFTER AGE 25 YOUR SEX DRIVE DECREASES and STOPS ALTOGETHER BY 65. Not true, and especially not for older women, whose skill and personal confidence often increase with age. Aging men do have physical changes but they do not decrease pleasure. Sex drive is as much a function of relational maturity and an available partner as it is of physical health and age.

IT IS THE MAN'S ROLE TO INITIATE SEX. This was an old cultural norm that pressured him to perform and relieved her of arousal guilt. It is now culturally acceptable for either or both partners to initiate, according to his or her own style, pace, and desire.

IF EITHER PARTNER IS AROUSED, INTERCOURSE MUST FOLLOW. This hints that people cannot or should not control sexual behavior (e.g., If he has an erection, he must ejaculate in his

partner. If she is aroused, she must orgasm or have cramps.).
Both can safely ignore the urge and enjoy the arousal, or they can
masturbate to orgasm alone or together. We *can* practice what we
ask of our adolescent children.

HAVING "G" SPOT AND MULTIPLE ORGASMS MEANS A
WOMAN IS SEXUALLY LIBERATED. Any woman is free to
experience bodily pleasures with her life partner. The fortunate
one has learned how to teach her partner about G-spot stimulation.
Sexual liberation means whatever you decide it means.

MENOPAUSE DECREASES SEXUAL DESIRE AND AROUSAL.
Decreasing estrogen levels raise, lower, or have no effect on desire
and arousal. This is a female mystery.

WHEN YOU LOSE SEXUAL DESIRE, THE BEST REMEDY IS
TO FIND ANOTHER PARTNER. This idea makes someone else
responsible for pushing you toward your sexual potential as though
you could not do this for yourself. The best (and hardest) remedy
is to honor yourself and your potential to mature in the relationship
you have.

A MAN WITH A BIG PENIS IS A HIGHLY SKILLED LOVER.
The size of a penis does not predict level of sexual energy or skill.
It may induce pride in its owner or, unfortunately, an unreasonable
expectation to "perform."

LARGE-BREASTED WOMEN ARE EASIER TO AROUSE
THAN SMALL-BREASTED WOMEN. Breast size is not a
measure of arousability. Some nipple tissue is arousable and some
not, and some is, some of the time. Size (amount of fatty tissue)
is not a factor in physical arousal, but the belief is. The belief can
influence your feeling desirable and, thus, your arousability.

MARRIED PEOPLE DO NOT MASTURBATE. Of course married people masturbate. They just do not discuss it in public and sometimes not even with each other. Masturbation is not a substitute for partner sex, it is legitimate sex-for-one. You can invite your partner to join you or observe you.

ONCE YOU KNOW THE SEXUAL ROPES, YOU ARE SET FOR LIFE. High school boys like to believe this. You are "set" only in that you can acknowledge you must learn each partner, again and again. This makes you a good learner and, thus, an acceptable lover in a physical sense.

THE BEST SEX IS SPONTANEOUS AND UNPLANNED. People without children, pets, or jobs may believe this. Even spontaneous sex is planned, for example, when you brush your teeth or wear certain underwear. The best sex is planned with happy anticipation by both partners. And, great unplanned sex happens, too.

PENIS-IN-VAGINA IS THE ONLY SEX THAT REALLY COUNTS. This misconception gives men performance anxiety and insinuates that a man is only as good as his erect, thrusting penis, and a woman, her open vagina.

THE BEST SEX IS WITH YOUR EYES CLOSED AND A SEXUAL FANTASY. Having a sexual fantasy connects you to your fantasy, not to your partner. Fantasies mostly distance partners. If closing your eyes disconnects you from your partner, look at, and be with, the real person. Note how anxious you get being this connected.

IF I DO NOT AROUSE MY PARTNER, I AM NOT PERFORM-ING AS I SHOULD. Although your partner's arousal and orgasm are not your responsibility, your own technical and relational skills are. If your partner is not aroused, find out why. Lack of arousal may have nothing at all, or everything, to do with your skill or presence. Need for approval or praise may be getting in your way. Genital performance should not be used for reassurance or evaluation. And "do" your partner for your own enjoyment and arousal, not as a duty.

SUCCESSFUL SEX MEANS I HAVE AN ORGASM EVERY TIME. Intimate, erotic sex is not goal oriented. Instead, its orientation is intense pleasure and the thrill of deep connection. Measuring sex in terms of "success" or "failure" dampens pleasure and fosters performance pressure. In fact, women and older men often do not have an orgasm with each sexual act, yet they enjoy the arousal. Factors such as age, maturity, stimulation, orgasm threshold, medication, physical or medical problems, depression, anxiety, and marital issues, for example, affect your orgasmic ability.

I wish my partner believed differently about:

I wish I believed differently about:

Wake-Up Calls

Partners leave a trail of wake-up calls for each other when they really mean they want the other to change. Everyone has effective and ineffective ways to request or refuse change. Sometimes it is hard to realize your attempts are ineffective. One mark of success is the ability to dialogue effectively about very tough issues, especially those about being disregarded. Wake-up calls can, when heeded, be transformed into personal insight, self-respect, increased closeness, and physical love. Uneasiness about discussing sexual issues prohibits the necessary dialogue and makes contact difficult.

Wake-up calls become self-defeating cycles when they are unheard or disregarded. Objectionable behavior does not disappear by itself no matter how long you ignore it. Blaming your partner is easier than looking at your own contributions to your circumstances. Listen well for quiet wake-up calls lest they escalate into affairs, passivity, defensiveness, nastiness, and absence.

A wake-up call, or warning, is a subtle or obvious tension that alerts you to something your partner wants you to know but may or may not say in words. Your response reflects your level of perception and willingness to engage in a different way, especially if the new way feels uncomfortable. Does emotional discomfort have a place in your relationship? Do you have effective ways to know each other? Is your relationship mostly a convenient place to replenish sex, money, food, laundry, security, or self-esteem?

There are many variations of wake-up calls, too many to name here, but a lengthy beginning starts this exercise. Warnings happen in every relationship; how you manage yourself in the face of their signals can wear you down or enhance your growth. For more in-depth information read *Why Marriages Succeed or Fail* by John Gottman (Suggested Readings, p. 103).

Suggestions:

1. Indicate which characteristics seem to fit you.

2. Check each characteristic that fits your partner.

3. Compare and discuss responses. Note how easily or reluctantly you contain your rebuttal, and notice how and whether you listen and hear.

4. When your partner is brave and honest enough to reveal self-defeating thoughts and behaviors, note how open and empathic you feel.

5. Don't explode, don't cave in, and don't leave. Just quiet yourself.

6. Afterwards, talk about what it was like to discuss your wake-up calls. (Hundreds of couples have voted this the second hardest exercise.)

Wake-up Calls and Warnings

Avoiding Contact

☐ No time for each other.

☐ No affectionate or sexual touching.

☐ No time for play, alone or together.

☐ Doing something more hours alone than together; one is dissatisfied with this arrangement.

☐ Longing for (or ignoring) an emotional connection with your partner while you fill time with someone else.

☐ No conversations, relaxation, insights, or projects together even if you want them.

☐ Spending time with chat rooms, internet sex, computer games, TV, hobbies, while ignoring your partner even when s/he does not complain.

☐ Sex is a bore, a chore, time-consuming, too anxiety-producing, or non-existent.

Ineffective Contact

☐ Being distant or aloof.

☐ Arguing, defending, criticizing.

☐ Condoning your partner's argumentativeness, defensiveness, or criticalness by similar behavior.

☐ Attacking as a way to relate when you are stressed, hurt, angry, disappointed, frustrated, etc.

☐ Blaming or shaming yourself or your partner.

☐ Escalating negativity and ignoring positives.

☐ Giving or receiving a silent simmer or helpless pout.

☐ Accepting the silent treatment without confronting it.

☐ Ignoring what you hear or know needs to change.

☐ Enabling your partner's passivity by ineffective confrontation or passive revenge.

☐ Withdrawing often as a way to relate.

☐ Complaining, threatening, or whining.

☐ Feeling helpless; thinking effective contact depends on the other person.

Insufficient Good Will

☐ Expressing or feeling contempt.

☐ Tolerating contempt instead of dealing with it.

☐ Being sarcastic, scathing, nasty, or mean.

☐ Tolerating sarcasm, hostility, nastiness, or meanness.

☐ Victimizing or disempowering you or your partner.

☐ Lying to your partner.

☐ Excusing the other one's lies.

☐ Hostile teasing.

☐ Pretending the hostile teasing doesn't hurt.

☐ Slapping, hitting, pinching, pushing, kicking, or any hurtful physical expression, accidental or intentional.

☐ Tolerating punishment of any kind.

☐ Expressing yourself in a way that demeans or violates your partner, and excusing your hurtful behavior.

Loss of Integrity

- [ ] Behaving dishonestly, then excusing yourself.

- [ ] Lying to yourself.

- [ ] Not feeling appropriately remorseful.

- [ ] Hiding your rejection instead of claiming it.

- [ ] Pretending you do not know what is dishonest, guilty, or rejecting, and excusing your or your partner's lack of integrity "for good reason" or "to keep the peace."

- [ ] Saying you agree when you don't, stifling your opinions to avoid unpleasantness or assure harmony.

- [ ] Accepting your partner's obligatory agreement.

- [ ] Overworking, overeating, overspending, gambling, drug use, and other behaviors that hurt someone.

- [ ] Ineffectively observing your partner's hurtfulness.

- [ ] Secrets about pornography, masturbation, affairs.

- [ ] Ignoring emotional absences and excuses.

- [ ] Exploding, caving in, spacing out, numbing, leaving.

- [ ] Tolerating your partner's explosions, caving in, spacing out, numbing, leaving.

Hints:

Accept your own and your partner's right to disagree and remain in relationship (in the same room at the same time).

Remember, you can ask you partner to change a behavior, but not an experience. Experience is not negotiable.

No matter who does what, neither partner is innocent.

Focus on, and express, your own experience.

Thinking you have no control over habitual, automatic reactions does not excuse you from containing yourself.

Act with more kindness and compassion than usual.

Do this even when your partner does not cooperate.

Know that an enemy has worth.

Choose integrity, self-respect, and good will ahead of comfort and security.

Tolerate your partner's growth.

Claiming your own part in creating your relationship is as essential as it can be awkward and embarrassing.

Manage the monumental challenge and inevitable anxiety that comes with getting what you yearn for.

Notes

Characteristics of Sexually Alive Couples

Hundreds of sexually alive couples, all midlife and older, listed for this handbook the particular characteristics they believe keep them sexual and exclusive. In the next exercise, you compare your own qualities with those of sexually active, intimate, mature, lifelong couples.

(Clarification: the term *monogamous* is a legal term that means married to one person. It does not imply fidelity or sexual exclusivity. Couples interviewed for handbook research were mostly sexually exclusive; that is, they had no consensually open marriages although some had had affairs, long ago, with productive resolution.)

The definition of *emotional maturity*, defined further in another section, is vital to the ideas here:

- Ability to define yourself with your partner
- Soothe your own anxiety
- Admit you are wrong when you are wrong
- Validate your own feelings and reality
- Manage insecurity, anxiety, and conflict
- Observe and regulate your own responses
- Stay connected to your partner
- Verify yourself as whole and separate
- All without exploding, caving in, or leaving.

You can clarify with your partner your own requirements for being or becoming more sexually alive. Consider how much and which qualities are yours that you would like to enhance. Note that, "love" and "romance" are not included in the following list.

Sexually alive couples speak their truth to each other, mostly with compassion. They manage their behavior and share hurt, anger, joy, fear, and other feelings that induce anxiety, shame, or fear. Having room to grow, they tolerate the results of that growth and then go through life enjoying and relishing each other for better and for worse. Their good will and respect shine through, even (or especially) when they disagree. Being in their company feels solid.

Suggestions:

1. Find enough time to be with your partner to discuss your reasons, if any, for being sexually exclusive.

2. Consider each quality on the list and discuss how this is, or is not, characteristic of your own way to relate. Do not develop a list about your partner.

3. Talk about the possible positive and negative effects of actually getting your heart's desire.

4. If you feel dead in your relationship, consider claiming that. Focus on your own deadness and your part in diminishing yourself or your relationship.

5. Don't explode, don't cave in, and don't leave. Just quiet yourself.

6. Take time to talk about what it was like for you to discuss the qualities that keep (or might keep) your relationship sexually alive.

Ten Characteristics of Sexually Alive Couples

☐ Sense of humor.

☐ More joy, play, and laughter than resentment.

☐ Respect for yourself and your partner.

☐ Frequent affectionate and sexual touch.

☐ Presence, being fully contact-able and response-able.

☐ Predictability, comfort, familiarity (Closeness).

☐ Unpredictability, anxiety, newness (Intimacy).

☐ Emotional separateness and togetherness.

☐ Responsibility for self-validation, self-soothing, self-awareness, autonomy, and choices (Maturity).

☐ Bringing whole self to the relationship in good faith with yourself and your partner (Integrity).

My own sexual aliveness includes:

Productive Disclosure

One of the more difficult conversations for couples is the one in which they say, or avoid saying, what is not happening sexually, especially if they feel frustrated or disappointed. "I don't want to hurt you." "I don't want to push you away." "I dread your reaction." "It's not your fault; it's just who I am." Partners protect each other from unwanted feelings with cheerful, impersonal discussion about nonthreatening topics. Speaking candidly is difficult but honest.

Talking personally about your real experience eliminates emotional walls and creates productive anxiety. Productive anxiety mobilizes you to activate your integrity. For example, instead of exploding, caving in, or leaving, you face your partner and speak for yourself with your own support. This can feel frightening if your habit is to lean on your partner for validation or approval. When productive anxiety spurs you to stand on your own with integrity and compassion, this is a "maturity spurt." Your partner may feel surprised, rejected, threatened, relieved, amused, or appreciative. You will feel self-respect and relief.

You demean your partner when you protect him or her from hearing a description of your experience. You demean yourself when you spill out your feelings without monitoring or managing them, as if you were not an adult in charge of your style of expression.

Making an agreement (with yourself) to say your piece with compassion goes a long way toward boosting your confidence and self-respect. Self-respect helps you focus on your own experience instead of your partner's faults and oversights. Talking tough and compassionately at the same time, about yourself, is important.

Many books on how to communicate are available if you want to refresh your skills, such as *Getting the Love You Want* and *Hot Monogamy* (see Suggested Readings. p. 103). Learn to listen without feeling devastated or getting your feelings bruised. Your partner's seemingly nasty intent is another way s/he expresses fear.

Sexual intimacy cannot advance without verbal, physical, and emotional contact. Productive disclosure encourages you to be fully present (open, honest, compassionate, self-disclosing, self-soothing, listening) with your partner. This is as crucial as physical touch because erotic sex requires full presence.

When your partner reveals himself or herself through self-disclosure, receive this gift-of-knowing whether or not you elect to use it in the service of enriching yourself and your relationship. Learn more about yourself as you focus on your partner's disclosure.

Suggestions:

1. Fill out the Disclosure Checklist by yourself.

2. Compare and discuss what you each have written.

3. Don't explode, don't cave in, and don't leave. Just quiet yourself.

4. When you have talked as much as you want, discuss what disclosing was like for you.

Productive Disclosure

1. When I feel anxious about being sexual with you, I:

2. Sometimes your touch feels:

3. I think I'm supposed to like everything we do sexually, but:

4. I truly love your touch when you:

5. I feel something special during sex when I:

6. When I feel "careful" during sex, I:

7. I wish I would change the way I:

8. If you could enjoy me more, I might:

9. If I could enjoy me more, I might:

10. If I could enjoy you more, I might:

11. I would turn on more intensely if I:

12. Sex is _____ right now; I wish I could:

13. What I want from you outside of bed is:

14. What I want from myself outside of bed is:

15. I can tell when your body is with me and your spirit is somewhere else, by:

16. I would like to get primitive and lustful when:

17. I'm concerned that you will/won't tell me if you dislike something, sexually, so I:

18. When I say what I dislike or want different, you:

19. Sex is/isn't fun for me because:

20. I sometimes pretend to have an orgasm so that:

21. When I get the nerve, I will talk about:

22. Here is what I really like about myself sexually:

Notes

Sexual Scripts

Each of us learns as a child how to behave in order to be acceptable to family, peers, and society. We receive serious spoken and unspoken rules about how to think, feel, and act according to adult social values. Parents, teachers, and others impose rules by etching values in young minds.

As children, we get "sexual scripts"—prescriptions we subconsciously store—for how not to be sexual. We carry these scripts with us to adulthood, where we still behave and feel (or we rebel and don't feel) as we were taught. The subconscious mind draws upon the old script for survival, even when there is no threat. Everybody carries scripts about sex and sexuality. Raising them from unconscious to conscious increases your choice to keep constructive ones and discard what no longer fits.

Uncovering your particular script and using that information to reinforce your sexual self can generate both relief and anxiety. Scripts, by definition hidden from consciousness, are uncovered through attention to your behavior, thoughts, and feelings and bridging present feelings and attitudes with those learned as a child. When you can acknowledge the old prescriptions, you have the option to change them to fit you. Restructuring your script requires awareness and courage.

The next exercise can help you observe your script. If you find a blind spot, ask for help, guess, or make up a response. If you do not know which ideas and values you received from parental figures, think about your present values and where or how they might have originated. Your present values reflect your acceptance or resistance to script messages.

Suggestions:

1. Privately, write or think about the next items.

2. Make enough time to discuss your responses. This information is private but not secret. Appreciate your partner's disclosures and listen with compassion, focus, and respect. Appreciate your own disclosure and speak with compassion, focus, and respect for yourself.

3. Don't explode, don't cave in, and don't leave. Just quiet yourself.

4. When you have shared as much as you can, talk about what discussing sexual scripts was like.

Sexual Script

1. Write a positive idea you received from your mother (or surrogate) about sex:

2. Write a positive idea you received from your father (or surrogate) about sex:

3. Write a negative idea you received from your mother (or surrogate) about sex:

4. Write a negative idea you received from your father (or surrogate) about sex:

5. How do these messages affect your sexuality now?

6. If you could change anything about your present sexual (or nonsexual) experience, how do you imagine yourself behaving differently?

7. How would you like your children (or others) to feel about their own sexuality?

Perspectives on Sex

Each generation has its own unique perspective on sexual skill, knowledge, behavior, attitude, and experience. Religions have guidelines about sex, communities have rules, families have jurisdiction, and peers have information, real and imaginary. It is no wonder so many of us grow up sexually confused. In the next exercise, you have an opportunity to expand your perspectives about sex.

The perspectives here are in two categories: conventional, meaning customary or standard, and unconventional, meaning uncommon or unique. Conventional perspectives are founded on romantic ideals of fulfilling dependency and security needs. Sex is viewed as natural rather than learned. Ideas of the biological urge to propagate overlap with the learned skills and techniques of sexual pleasure. Standard notions imply that sex, like hunger, is an appetite. Without a hunger for sex, you are labelled "sexually anorexic" rather than "overcome with integrity." Western culture fosters romance and co-dependency: "If you love me and take care of me I will never leave you, and I promise not to grow up." *Avoiding* sexual problems under these circumstances would be surprising, indeed.

The unconventional perspective is based on maturity (self-respect), integrity (wholeness), intimacy (self-connection), and the idea that good sex happens with a feeling of fullness, not neediness. In most media portrayals, mature love is unconventional or unseen. We rarely see or read the results of partners soothing and validating themselves effectively instead of expecting the other to provide comfort. Rarely, if ever, does the paradox come up that emotional separateness and self-sufficiency help you bond *more intimately*, not less. The reality, according to hundreds of sexually active couples, is that integrity and maturity are lasting and effective aphrodisiacs. The uncommon view is that, while reproductive sex is biologically determined, lifelong erotic sex with the same partner develops over time, with effort.

Suggestions:

1. Find time to do this exercise together. Read each concept from both perspectives and talk about what each one means to you, personally and relationally. Items from both perspectives will fit.

2. As you discuss the meaning of each concept, note how similar or different your thoughts are, whether you soothe yourself, manage anxiety, and monitor your automatic reactions.

3. Don't explode, don't cave in, and don't leave. Just quiet yourself. Hear and honor a perspective different from yours.

4. When you have shared as much as you agreed to, for now, take time to discuss what talking about different sexual perspectives was like for you.

Perspectives on Sex

A Conventional, Familiar Perspective

☐ Sex is a natural hunger.

☐ "I'm faithful to you so you *owe me* sex and fidelity."

☐ Focus is on genitals, techniques, positions, sex-toys.

☐ Have a fantasy instead of tuning in to your partner.

☐ Desire is a function of needing sex.

☐ For good sex, reduce anxiety, relax, get comfortable.

☐ Arousal should happen with minimal physical stimulation, especially for men.

☐ Passion gradually subsides over time.

☐ Avoid (or expect partner to fix) a sexual problem.

☐ Partners validate, assure, and protect each other.

☐ Security depends on a partner's behavior and mood.

☐ Emotional security overrides integrity and honesty.

☐ The main complaint is, "I'm not getting what I want from my partner in this relationship."

An Unconventional, Unfamiliar Perspective

☐ Good sex happens with fullness, not need.

☐ "Faithfulness comes from an agreement I make with myself. It is not negotiable with promises."

☐ Focus is often on intimate erotic connection.

☐ Tune in your partner, tolerate mutual erotic energy, no need for fantasy.

☐ Desire happens before, during, and after sex, a function of want, not need.

☐ Tolerate and manage the anxiety of high arousal.

☐ Arousal occurs with profound, erotic stimulation.

☐ Passion for your partner increases with your ability to tolerate anxiety and manage insecurity.

☐ Talk about problems, they are fertile opportunities.

☐ Validate, reassure yourself, create your own safety.

☐ Security depends on awareness and self-soothing.

☐ Emotional security is a result of self-responsibility.

☐ The main complaint is, "I'm not getting what I want from myself in this relationship."

Conversations about Sex

Do you remember a time early in your relationship when you talked for hours, told each other everything, and believed you would always be self-revealing and lusty? That was the "in love" stage when hormones and chemistry overcame all obstacles, and communication was not an issue.

When you grew to know each other better, maturity allowed you to encounter disappointment, frustration, disillusionment, and still remain connected. Had you stayed happy with each other the way you were, you would not have developed into *sexually* mature adults. A reward of discontent is making room for growth. Instead of trying to whip your partner into shape, you take on the task of improving yourself. Communication is not the issue, you did not forget how. The problem comes when neither wants to hear what the other has to say; it exposes or hides too much.

Couples who can communicate skillfully often do not talk effectively about sexual issues. The focus may be children, finances, in-laws, etc., to the exclusion of the delicate sex topic. However, managing an awkward conversation is good practice for boosting erotic energy. Erotic sex is simply an ability to balance high sexual arousal with high anxiety with a life partner and tip the scale in favor of your own lustiness.

The next exercise can help you re-experience each other through guided conversations about sex. You can have similar conversations about other issues by substituting money, children, or whatever, for "sex." Be responsible for your intent and do the exercise to completion.

51

Suggestions:

1. Make time to be together for this exercise. Write or discuss each statement as you read aloud.

2. Take turns talking about each statement after you read it. Note whether this is easy, difficult, fun, boring, nostalgic, sad, irritating, scary, etc. Tell your partner the truth about *your* experience. Pat yourself on the back if you balance your excitement with your anxiety.

3. Don't explode, don't cave in, and don't leave. Just quiet yourself. Stay present with your partner. Note your unease out loud if you have any, and manage it as you talk with your partner.

4. When you have finished discussing responses, review out loud what you noticed about yourself and how you felt while you talked about conversations about sex.

Conversations about Sex

1. I appreciate you sexually in this relationship for:

2. One of your qualities I find most attractive is:

3. I chuckle every time I think about:

4. A deeply tender moment with you, sexually, was:

5. A tough time for me sexually was/is:

6. What I learned from that about myself:

7. If I had a year left to live, I would want:

8. If you had a year left to live, I would want:

9. I depend on you for:

10. Three ways to be together we both might enjoy:

11. When we first got together sexually I hoped:

12. My hope for the future:

13. I feel most open and willing to have a sexually revealing conversation with you when I:

14. What I feel (think/want) sexually for now.

Dysfunctional, Functional, and Intimate Sex

The usual view of sexual behavior offers only two categories, dysfunctional and functional. These classifications refer to your plumbing, not your loving. Using only two measures to evaluate sexual behavior ignores intimate sex and the deeply erotic love *experience* between life partners.

Intimate and erotic sex happens between people who want (and can tolerate) more than functional, adequate, or boring sex. Although these partners may use erotica for an occasional variation, they rarely attempt to juice up sex with erotic videos, fantasies, and sex toys (all of which help until they become boring, too). Instead, they have the capacity to tolerate and transform productive anxiety into exciting, intimate loving, and erotic sex.

What kind of sex is not eventually monotonous? The kind that can simultaneously fill you with joy and fear, desire and anxiety, anticipation and dread. This kind of sex is generative as it erases destructive self-talk and tolerates erotic feelings and sensations. You can discover that anxiety is productive instead of lethal.

To shift from self-defeating to constructive attitudes through self-observation and intentional change is not boring. Nerve-wracking, yes, but not boring. Creating change by bringing something new of yourself to your relationship each day makes for sex (and life) that is rarely, if ever, monotonous. Mature people avoid monotonous sex and boring relationships by continuously generating stimulation about life and growth. They like to see each other grow, even when they feel nervous about it.

With a stay-comfortable contract, life feels safe and dull. By withstanding the anxiety of unpredictable, novel, emotionally uncomfortable behavior, nothing you experience, including sex, is boring for long. Mature couples actually have as many problems, sexual and otherwise, as others, but they see problems as opportunities for personal and relational growth, even if it causes temporarily uncomfortable or frighteningly emotional moments.

Suggestions:

1. Make time to do this exercise together. Read aloud to compare responses.

2. This exercise separates your mature self from your dependent self. As a competent adult, you can reveal your experience as you don't explode, don't cave in, don't leave, and do quiet yourself.

3. When you have finished the exercise, discuss what it was like to talk about the differences between dysfunctional, functional, and intimate sex.

Compare These Statements To Your Relationship:

Dysfunctional Sex:

☐ Chemistry is missing.

☐ Arousal is partial or absent.

☐ Orgasms are absent or puny.

☐ Physical response is insufficient.

☐ Desire for partner is low/absent.

☐ General disinterest prevails.

☐ One of the partners carries the problem.

☐ A sexual problem maintains the stability of the relationship.

☐ You both ignore signals for change.

☐ Sexual energy threatens security.

☐ Anxiety is not tolerated.

☐ Each wants the other to provide comfort and protection.

Functional Sex:

☐ Chemistry is mediocre or boring except on vacation.

☐ Arousal is utilitarian, obligatory, or fantasy-dependent.

☐ Orgasms are relaxing, low arousal, often fantasy-dependent.

☐ Physical response is adequate but rarely with passion.

☐ Desire is utilitarian, for release.

☐ Partners can take it or leave it.

☐ No problem noticed, just boredom.

☐ Comfort maintains the status quo.

☐ Neither risks consequences of change.

☐ Sexual energy is confined to special events and vacations.

☐ Anxiety is not well tolerated.

☐ Each comforts the other to avoid anxiety.

Intimate and Erotic Sex:

☐ Chemistry is present and changing.

☐ Arousal is often erotic, occasionally mediocre, rarely dull.

☐ Orgasms are intense, high arousal from being together, no fantasies needed.

☐ Physical response is intact.

☐ Desire is for partner, not for release.

☐ Partners still interest each other.

☐ Problems have meaning and potential to spur growth.

☐ Discomfort shifts the status quo.

☐ Both appreciate and accept change.

☐ Sexual expression is easier as partners mature.

☐ Anxiety is managed and used to grow on.

☐ Each soothes his or her own anxiety and tolerates the other's.

For in-depth information, read *Passionate Marriage* by David Schnarch, Ph.D. (see Suggested Readings, p. 103).

Notes

Closeness and Intimacy

Partners thrive on closeness (comfort, familiarity, predictability). Best friends often make excellent life partners for this reason. They care and know each other so well that they often predict with accuracy each other's thoughts, feelings, and behaviors. This makes for a familiar, comfortable, and stable relationship.

Intimacy is different from closeness. Intimacy is not comfortable because each moment brings new, unfamiliar, unpredictable experience and anxiety. To people uneasy with the unknown, intimacy feels very risky. To risk the unknown, you first have a strong sense of who you are and a certainty that you will not lose your sense of self even if you merge sexually with your partner.

Consider adding to your perspective of intimacy the idea that it means connecting deeply with yourself. To surrender to your unease as you let the best and the worst of yourself be known, you must be able to soothe yourself. Closeness allows you to know your partner better; intimacy allows you to know yourself better.

Making love with a life partner who, at the moment, is strange, new, and unpredictable, results in anxiety as well as excitement. To relish the moment, you must be able to delve into the strong, mature, self-soothing aspect of you that can tolerate or even enjoy unpredictability, strangeness, newness. This novel and uncertain nature of intimacy makes it a lifelong and reliable aphrodisiac.

Intimate moments—strange, novel, exciting—are so intense that people must cushion them with closeness, predictability, and comfort. Just as intimate moments are fostered by knowing yourself, closeness is fostered by knowing your partner. Malone and Malone in *The Art of Intimacy* (see Suggested Readings,

p. 103) put forth the idea that closeness and intimacy are different experiences.

You are the most deeply connected to yourself when you are feeling intimate with your partner. Mature couples can flow between closeness and intimacy: between feeling safe and risking being known, between feeling comfort and managing anxiety, between appreciating the predictable and accepting the unknown. For adults, knowing the difference between feeling unsafe and actually being in danger of losing your life, health, or integrity, is an important distinction. You know you are safe or you leave and call the police. It is difficult to know and be known sexually and intimately at the same moment when feeling safe and being safe are not clear in your mind. Effort is required to put love and sex together years after you have grown to know each other.

Suggestions:

1. Read the next exercise together. Discuss whether it fits and distinguish between your different attitudes.

2. Don't blow up, don't cave in, and don't leave. Just quiet yourself.

3. Talk about what it was like to consider how closeness and intimacy differ in your relationship.

Closeness is...

Familiar, comfortable, and predictable.

Affirming and sustaining your partner.

Partners who validate, affirm, and support each other.

When your primary awareness is your partner's thoughts and feelings.

When your partner is slightly more important to you than you are to yourself.

Experiencing your partner in shared space.

Intense interpersonal awareness of your relationship to your partner.

Partners caring for and complementing each other.

Gladly giving up portions of personal space and options to know your partner more deeply.

Negotiable because it is mostly about behavior and comfort, both of which are negotiable.

Knowing your partner.

Intimacy is...

Unfamiliar, risky, surprising.

Affirming and sustaining yourself.

Self-validating, self-affirming, self-supportive.

Being yourself without stopping your partner from being who s/he is; accepting her or him as is.

Relinquishing no part of yourself even though it is hard to be fully you with the person you depend on.

Experiencing yourself deeply with your partner.

Intense personal awareness of yourself.

Experiencing yourself in profound ways, not necessarily at the same time as your partner.

Being willing to change, grow, and tolerate anxiety, yours and your partner's.

Choosing to be compassionately truthful with yourself and your partner, staying related as you do.

Not negotiable because experience is not negotiable.

Knowing yourself.

Purposeful Sexual Partnerships

The key word in this exercise is "purposeful." The purpose, however, is not to help your partner be the person to whom you thought you committed yourself. Your purpose is to accept your partner, as is.

That leaves the changing to you. The objective of this exercise is for you to notice yourself, note the kind of person you want to be in relationship with your partner.

"But I can't be the kind of partner I want to be until my partner is the kind of person I need her or him to be."

This stance cheats you of being in charge of yourself. As an adult, you are, every moment, the partner and individual you choose to be. You can be compassionate, passive or rebellious. Neither permission nor approval from your partner can change who you are.

When you are clear about who you are and how you shall be with (and without) your partner, you are in charge, effective, and responsible for yourself. You are the person you want to be when you are being most yourself instead of who others seemingly pressure you to be. Being fully yourself with integrity takes precedence over keeping the peace. Harmony, like comfort and behavior, is negotiable, but keeping the peace at all costs sacrifices your integrity. Integrity means wholeness. Giving away a piece of yourself (e.g., keeping quiet for the sake of harmony) fragments you and sacrifices wholeness.

Being loving and sexual requires self-awareness. The next exercise offers another opportunity to practice being more fully aware and supportive of yourself. It's a chance to build your sexual relationship by developing yourself to like who you are when you are with your partner.

You are asked to select one of five options for the statements on the next pages:

"never," "rarely," "sometimes," "frequently," or "always."

You may dislike some of the statements, but discuss them anyway. Note how willingly you observe your own behavior and your partner's.

Suggestions:

1. Fill out the exercise individually, then compare.

2. Note discrepancies. If you think you do something "always" and your partner says "never," you are on fertile ground.

3. Note agreements. Appreciate them and move on; discrepancies promote growth.

4. Don't explode, don't cave in, and don't leave. Just quiet yourself.

5. When you have finished the exercise, discuss how it was for you to talk about purposeful sexual partnership building.

Purposeful Sexual Partnerships

1. I actively listen to my partner when s/he talks.

    never   rarely   sometimes   frequently   always

2. I behave respectfully even when I don't want sex.

    never   rarely   sometimes   frequently   always

3. I make appointments to express sexual frustration.

    never   rarely   sometimes   frequently   always

4. I occasionally engage my partner with sexual enthusiasm, play, and laughter.

    never   rarely   sometimes   frequently   always

5. I make time for sex, just us, alone somewhere.

    never   rarely   sometimes   frequently   always

6. I rarely criticize or withdraw after we have sex.

    never   rarely   sometimes   frequently   always

7. I stay present, clear, and handle my sexual anxiety.

    never   rarely   sometimes   frequently   always

8. During and after an argument about sex, I stay present until we clear the air or set another time.

    never   rarely   sometimes   frequently   always

9. I feel deeply connected to myself and my partner before, during, and after sex.

    never   rarely   sometimes   frequently   always

10. When my partner feels emotional about sex, I am present and responsive.

    never   rarely   sometimes   frequently   always

11. When my partner gets on my nerves about sex, I discuss it.

    never   rarely   sometimes   frequently   always

12. We engage in nonsexual projects together.

    never   rarely   sometimes   frequently   always

13. We both live with/without sexual energy and wonder how we created this.

    never   rarely   sometimes   frequently   always

Sexual Style

We don't think much about sexual style as another royal road to the unconscious. Yet, the pattern of your sexual style is communication, intended or not. Sexual style is founded on behavior that repeatedly blocks or supports intimacy and sexual enjoyment. While you can rest assured your subconscious will always see to your survival, you may be embarrassed to discover how you create a sexual style in your relationship without quite knowing how or why.

Like personality, everyone has a sexual style whether or not they have a sex partner. Sexual style may or may not mimic personality style. For example, an indecisive, passive person might be assertive sexually. A determined, dominating person might be sexually shy. Seemingly more often, styles follow the same patterns in and out of bed (or wherever you have sex). This means a chronically angry or suspicious person is not going to be a generous, sensitive lover; a gentle, considerate person is probably not going to turn selfish and demanding in bed.

The few hours before sexual activity occurs can reveal how a pattern begins and what happens next with both partners' behavior. A characteristic way of giving or receiving an invitation for sex might include, for example, being playful, enthusiastic, hesitant, reserved, funny, aggressive, passive, seductive, romantic, leading, following, expressive, self-confident, teasing, quiet, inviting, etc. Or, it might include being anxious, hostile, mean, sadistic, masochistic, tricky, pitiful, fearful, guilt-ridden, pleasureless, self-serving, etc.

The way you approach foreplay describes your sexual style and may suggest how you relate in other areas. Fear and shame can stir you in all areas of life. For example, fear of shame, punishment, rejection, neglect, intrusion, etc., can extinguish or inhibit sexual initiation and desire (not counting people aroused by sadomasochistic rituals). Whether you expect pleasure or pain from sex reveals your outlook about your relationship as much as about sex. Foreplay is an interaction that directs what happens next.

Examples of foreplay style include: giving, receptive, skilled, smooth, lusty, tentative, conventional, imaginative, persistent, reliable, conscientious, dramatic, leisurely, sensitive, assertive. Behaviors and attitudes we can learn to change can include: indifference, selfishness, caution, inhibition, aversion, aloofness. Observing the effect of your behavior on yourself and your partner is a useful tool for change. Foreplay, and those behaviors in which you no longer engage, is a message about the meaning of sex. Meaning *makes* foreplay.

Foreplay and intercourse are not only skills, they are physical expressions of what you want your partner to know about you. Intercourse style might include being endearing, lascivious, spontaneous, erotic, fun, serious, talkative, primitive, adventurous, irreverent, tender, loving, creative, juicy, insatiable, uniting, soulful. Behaviors to change might include being compliant, obligatory, dutiful, vigilant, intimidating, insistent, coercive, manipulative, disconnecting, distancing, and abusive. Your sexual behavior, like it or not, mirrors a message, often hidden from both of you, that invites your partner to guess what you mean. When you are aware, you can be intentional about being sexual.

We invariably find a partner whose sexual style pushes sexual growth. Maturing partners find this push fruitful rather than intolerable. Consequences of childhood socialization, loving or abusive, inevitably surface in long-term relationships. Childhood fears (if you are aware of any) can be managed by purposefully engaging your competent adult self when you notice them or feel afraid. Your competent adult self knows, or can learn, to struggle effectively with unproductive anxiety. Thus, you manage your anxiety from a place of competence. Otherwise, you default to your partner to take care of it for you. If you default, even temporarily, be certain it is to the partner who loves you, not an imaginary, malevolent partner. Sex, if you look closely enough, will reflect what is and is not taking place between partners.

Your partner either will or will not deal with anxiety as you improve yourself. Emotional security does not require you to protect your partner from your or his/her anxiety, give up your sense of self, compromise your integrity, or embrace helplessness. When you comfort your anxious or scared partner instead of simply being there, you cheat him or her of self-soothing and self-monitoring. This is a hard but necessary choice if you want erotic, sexual intimacy.

Your natural sexual self may be buried under layers and years of socialization. Reclaiming your right to feel your sexuality moves you into your adult, in-charge self, often with anxious relief. As a competent adult, you manage anxiety during, before, and after sex; and, you can share your experience with your partner. The blessing here is that your dissatisfaction motivates you to acknowledge what you want and go after it, even in the face of anxiety, because as an adult you have that choice.

Suggestions:

1. Create with your partner a list of words to describe your respective characteristic styles.

2. Note how you are alike and different. Talk about how styles affect your sexual energy. Talk about what your styles mean to you about yourselves.

3. Create on paper a map of a sexual encounter you would like to change or enhance. The idea is to find a pattern, then discuss how you can enhance or restructure it. Notice whether your discussion focuses on your own growth or your partner's.

4. Don't explode, don't cave in, and don't leave. Just quiet yourself.

5. Discuss what it was like to talk about your own sexual style and pattern of relating sexually.

Sexual Style

Mine   Yours

Patterns of Sexual Behavior

(Use the words you listed on the previous page.)

1. The first thing that happens is:

2. And then:

3. Here's how I predictably respond:

4. Here's how you predictably respond:

5. I do my predictable part anyway, because:

6. If I change the way I respond, then:

7. I would change this if:

Maturity

Because the term "maturity" has so many meanings, it works best to design your own definition. Knowing what maturity *means* in your relationship can give you sexual options, believe it or not. Maturity does not mean boring, grown-up, unsexy behavior. It means you are in charge of your life and responsible for the rewards and consequences of your behavior whether you are resting, playing, working, or just being you. Here's how you might benefit from defining maturity for yourself:

1. Maturity is the quality that helps you avoid compliance, defiance, and indecision (about sex and other choices).

2. Maturity is vital to erotic sex because it helps you tolerate yearning for what you don't have, gives you courage to go for what you want, and equips you with the freedom to accept or reject what you receive in response.

3. Maturity gives you the self-support to speak your truth, knowing it will push your partner and yourself to contain and manage the habit of knee-jerk reactions. You grow each time you use your competent adult self to contain your urge to defend, criticize, refute, or withdraw.

4. Maturity helps you avoid no-growth/no-change unspoken agreements and accept growth and change even (or especially) when it feels threatening.

5. Maturity gives you integrity, options, and resources to develop yourself instead of focusing on your partner's deficits and trying to whip her or him into shape. Mature awareness draws positive sexual energy to you.

"Do you have to have a partner to develop maturity?"

No, but a partner will push your growth in almost every way you have unknowingly avoided your whole adult life.

By now you should be familiar with one definition of maturity: "Don't explode, don't cave in, don't leave, just quiet yourself." This means you contain but do not stifle your feelings, and you listen actively. Containing your reaction lets you hear with intent and purpose, nonreactively, what your partner is trying to put across to you. You control your impulses instead of letting your impulses control you. Restrain yourself from your urge to interrupt or space out, in favor of listening to your partner's words, feelings, and intent *because you want to*, not because you're "supposed to" or "have to." Teach yourself to *want to*. Consider your partner's message and value it, even when you disagree. Arguing may be easier than listening actively and less threatening than being tender, but it creates nonintimate or even callous contact.

Suggestions:

1. Make time to read and discuss the statements on the next page. Add your own favorite characteristics.

2. Discuss how you might enrich your own maturity and what this might mean to your self-respect.

3. Restrain yourself from reminding your partner how to develop further. Focus on yourself and your own growing opportunities, not your partner's.

4. Don't explode, don't cave in, and don't leave. Just quiet yourself.

5. When you have completed the exercise to your own satisfaction, talk about what it was like to define maturity and predict ways your relationship might change if you added or enriched yours.

Notes

Maturity is the ability to:*

- Soothe your own anxiety, fear, and insecurities.

- Maintain your own identity in the face of pressure to conform to someone else's idea of how you should be.

- Tolerate your partner's intense emotions.

- Avoid protecting your partner from intense feelings.

- Tolerate risk, ambivalence, and contradictions.

- Manage dissatisfaction and change.

- Stand apart as separate individuals even as you value your togetherness.

- Set your own limits with consideration for, rather than responsibility for, your partner.

- Enjoy your partner more than you enjoy your children.

- Share the best and the worst of yourself.

- Look inside, tolerate what you see, and let each other in.

- Be of good will in words and actions.

- Play together.

- Receive and give love and respect.

- Balance yourself when you are pulled off-center.

- Tolerate joy, grief, anger, fear, and orgasm.

*With special appreciation to Drs. Murray Bowen, Joen Fagan, Thomas Malone, John Warkentin, and Carl Whitaker.

Notes

Contradiction and Paradox

Contradiction and paradox are normal, useful, everyday life workings. A contradiction is an opposing, contrary, or conflicting opinion; a paradox is a statement or idea that is contrary to popular belief but that might actually be true. Both help people come to terms with their differences and separateness, both present opportunities for sexual growth.

Contradictions cause conflict useful for expanding your thinking. Managing conflict is also necessary for personal growth. "Managing" does not mean stifle yourself or defer "to keep the peace." Managing contradiction and paradox means you bring together conflicting ideas or seemingly opposite beliefs. To see the contradiction from a higher vantage point, you view one side as a possibility. Then, you view the other side as equally plausible. Making them into another, comprehensively different whole, is what mature, sexually active couples do, together.

For example, the statement, "I want my partner to have sex with me, but I feel trapped by her or his desire," is a fertile contradiction that allows, or requires, self-observation and conscious choice. Is "being desired" or "wanting sex" tolerable? Who imposes feeling "trapped?" Einstein said that you cannot solve the problem on the level of the problem. This means you rise above the problem to see the whole picture. For this example, feeling trapped is a function of what you tell yourself, not of your partner's behavior or desire, as it may seem.

"I want an intimate relationship where I control what happens." The contradiction is that intimacy and emotional control do not exist side-by-side. In sexual relationships, emotional intimacy

81

happens between peers, not between people who control or tolerate being controlled.

Conscious control of yourself elevates you from a dependent stance. Being accountable to yourself, claiming responsibility for yourself, and doing this in relationship with your partner shifts you into genuineness. "I want an intimate relationship where I am in control of *me*," is a statement of authenticity and possibility. In relationship language, this means you value your perspective and your partner's perspective whether or not you agree. Creating "both and" instead of "either or" choices eliminates power struggles without erasing personal power.

Suggestions:

1. Read the next exercise with your partner. Uncover individual and relational contradictions. Notice how easy or difficult it is to bring seemingly opposite sides of a question together.

2. Don't explode, don't cave in, and don't leave. Just quiet yourself.

3. When you have finished the exercise, talk about what it was like to discuss your individual and relational contradictions.

Using Contradictions

I Want...	And I also want...
To be close.	Solitude.
Self-reliance.	Dependability.
To love unconditionally.	To honor my love conditions.
To be loved and desired by my partner.	Bigger planetary concerns than if I am desired.
To develop myself.	Growth to occur relationally.
Self-awareness and autonomy.	Suggestions and guidance.
To live in the moment.	To plan for the future.
Oneness with my partner.	To be separate and individual.
To work for harmony.	Some rest from all this work.
Passion and intensity.	Friendship and reliability.
Sexual arousal and connection.	Companionship, peace, quiet.
To do all of this yesterday; life is too short to waste even one moment.	There is enough time for this; life is to be savored a little at a time.

Notes

Thoughts about Sex

Some thoughts about sex are easier to grasp than others. The next pages are assorted ideas shared by mental health professionals and other sexually active couples having juicy sex, some for 50 years and still going strong. We can apply their guidelines to our own growing relationships. They tell us about staying sexually alive for life, genitally and otherwise, based on their personal development.

Increasing your sexual intensity (after the "falling-in-love" stage ends) happens as you experience what love and sex *means* with your partner. Experiencing meaning is different from mentally understanding an idea. Meaning is what gives you a positive experience in relationship, the one with yourself as well as the one with your partner. Talking about what sex means to you, what being in relationship with this particular person means to you, giving meaning to your everyday interactions, these are beneficial discussions to have periodically, not just during courtship.

For example, knowing the significance of your relationship to your living helps you find meaning. Seeking judgment as a sexual partner does not help you find meaning. Thinking about your "performance" is another way of searching for approval and reassurance, not meaning. Needing acceptance will not help you become erotic; your need focuses your attention on your partner's opinion, not on your experience. Thus, the very idea of "performance" leads to getting your need for approval met. The meaning of love and sex in your relationship is to express your love, joy, desire, and respect for your partner and yourself.

Playfulness and sensuality mixed with sexual contact, not reassurance or need, lends meaning through self-expression deeply felt. Maturity allows playfulness without self-consciousness, which is, paradoxically, a gift from your child-self. This helps you find meaning in your sexuality.

Your experience of meaning is more than understanding the significance of your and your partner's behavior. It is being fully present with yourself while you are physically near your partner so that you "get" the connection deep in your bones. You know it, your partner knows, and you know s/he knows. Such profound knowing is discomforting and awesome.

Suggestions:

1. Read the next page aloud with your partner. Discuss the notions and your understanding of them.

2. Don't explode, don't cave in, and don't leave. Just quiet yourself.

3. When you have finished, discuss what it was like for you to talk about these particular ideas.

A Collection of Thoughts about Sex

1. Unlike reproductive, ordinary, or casual sex, erotic sex is developed over time between mature partners.

2. You deepen your ability to love each time you see the other person clearly and accept who he or she is aside from your own needs, wants, and beliefs.

3. If you love yourself, you invite intimacy instead of attachment hunger into your life.

4. In a loving relationship you feel good about yourself most of the time.

5. Most socially polite people behave only as erotically as they believe their partner can tolerate.

6. Attention and compassion are effective aphrodisiacs.

7. Intense genital stimulation and orgasm are not sufficient for erotic sex.

8. Compliant and obligatory sex lead eventually to sexual apathy and resentment in both partners.

9. Sexual apathy is often an unspoken plea for presence when one or both partners is not mindfully there.

10. No matter what or whom the complaint is about, neither partner is innocent.

11. Until you can affirm yourself, you cannot be fully erotic and intimate.

12. You must utilize considerable self-observation, self-soothing, and self-support in erotic, intimate loving.

13. Sexually exclusive behavior (erroneously thought of as "monogamy") is a personal decision based on integrity, self-respect, and fairness. Sexual exclusivity is a vow you make to yourself.

14. Loving, wanting, and receiving love require you to acknowledge and tolerate the impermanence and loss of a relationship and a beloved partner.

15. In a life partnership, one of you will eventually mourn the death of the other. You can choose an intimate, erotic relationship and suffer that devastating loss once, or you can lose it a little each day that you choose comfort over intimacy.

With deep appreciation for personal communication over many years to unnamed lifelong couples and: Drs. Lee Blackwell, O. Spurgeon English, Joen Fagan, Richard E. Felder, Vivian Guze, Elaine L. Levin, Alexander Jasnow, Howard M. Halperin, Kitty La Perriere, Thomas P. Malone, Natasha Mann, Frances and Bill Nagata, Augustus Y. and Margaret Napier, David M. Schnarch, Sol and Bernice Rosenberg, John Warkentin, and Carl A. Whitaker.

Sexual Potential

Sexual potential is the mental, emotional, physical, and spiritual level to which you can aspire sexually. An individual limit ("glass ceiling") can prevent you from reaching your full sexual potential. The level at which your "glass ceiling" stops your progress depends on your ability to soothe yourself, tolerate anxiety, manage pressure to conform, observe and use conflict and contradiction, and hold fast to your identity when pressed to be different. In other words, your maturity. Reaching for sexual potential requires you to acknowledge your partner and yourself as whole beings, not defectives who need to change.

You raise your "glass ceiling" as you mature. If you have experienced the handbook exercises more or less in order, you have some idea of what maturity means to you and your partner and how that fits your relationship. To approach your sexual potential, you determine where and how your "glass ceiling" stops you from expressing yourself sexually. Fortunately, the "ceiling," your erotic energy cap, has nothing whatsoever to do with your partner; rather, it is a figment of your own creation.

"Well, OK, but how does a person manage his or her own maturity and sexuality in a relationship?"

Caringly, not carefully. You affirm ownership of your own mind, body, soul, and desire to connect with your partner mindfully, physically, and soulfully. The "glass ceiling" is your challenge to yourself to claim responsibility for your own thoughts, feelings, and behaviors. When you do, you have resources with which to enhance, enrich, and change whatever no longer serves your growth or your relationship, independent of your partner's choices and opinions. You then learn how to live with the resulting change (or lack thereof) in your partner.

Pushing your sexual relationship forward can feel risky. You have more to lose when you feel loving and juicy rather than dull and dead with your partner, especially if you have reached midlife and beyond. Having little or no energy for your relationship minimizes your suffering when your partner leaves or dies. On the other hand, while you are both alive, you are both deprived of loving feelings. Risking deep feelings for your partner, especially sexual feelings, means the possibility for a loving, erotic relationship for the duration, however brief.

By approaching your sexual potential with integrity and maturity, you can discover the experience that happens after you quiet yourself (you know, the last part of, "Don't explode, don't cave in, don't leave..."). You let your partner in. You move your sexual energy forward, sometimes together, right through the glass ceiling. You will have the maturity to reinvent sacred sex in your own relationship. This is the real journey toward intimacy.

Suggestions:

1. Read the next page to yourself. Notice which descriptions fit you and discuss your responses. If you think, "I could feel more sexual if only my partner would do or be such and such..." focus on the aspect of your living for which you can claim responsibility without needing your partner to behave a certain way. Depending on each other's behavior, mood, or opinion (instead of your own) for your choices is a clear signal that growth is imminent, especially if one of you is dissatisfied about something.

2. Don't explode, don't cave in, and don't leave.   Just quiet yourself.

3. When you have finished, discuss what it was like to talk about sexual potential.

Notes

Approaching Sexual Potential Includes:

☐ Willingness to be responsible to yourself, without pretense, with your partner, including sexually.

☐ The capacity to be caught off guard and enjoy the surprise and novelty.

☐ The ability to find fresh possibilities in familiar surroundings.

☐ The occasional longing for the presence *and* absence of your partner.

☐ The ability to play, be curious, be creative.

☐ Valuing your integrity so you can eliminate useless childhood warnings about sex and heal the wounds of sexual abuse.

☐ The ability to observe and tolerate anxiety, ambivalence, and contradictions.

☐ Willingness to risk being coupled in new ways.

☐ Accepting the unchangeable rhythms and cycles of life.

☐ Acknowledging impermanence and loss, yet loving deeply anyway.

Notes

Practicing Loss

Nobody likes to do this exercise; it is number one on the most unfavorite list. It is also number one in eye-opening for people willing to risk having the kind of relationship that can handle erotic intimacy.

It is painful to anticipate the loss of your partner and your relationship as you know it, to think about being alone after decades of living with a beloved person. Yet, being mindful of life's inevitable endings can urge you toward planning your future, and more important, your present. The rewards of the present are as sweet as the pain of the future will be bitter. We hope for bittersweet memories instead of bitterness for experience not tasted. You can decide at any time to be the partner you want to be in the relationship you have, and spend your remaining time together with purpose.

Practicing loss includes thinking about life without your partner. Death is inescapable. Denying its inevitability cheats you of living life fully in the present. You can plan for the eventuality or pretend to have the time you want; however, either way has important consequences. Valuing your partner and your time together now and planning for a predictable future are developmental tasks whatever your age and however much time you *think* you have left.

If you are over fifty, think about the next decades and how you want to spend them with your partner. Think about growing old together and what that means to you. Then think about growing old alone, and how you might manage emotionally and socially. Will you move forward in your own living and loving? How will you survive the tragedy of your loss? Do you have a place in the hearts of friends and family? Do they have a place in your heart? Do you know where insurance papers are kept? The toilet paper stored?

If you are under fifty, think about what the next years might bring if your partner were to die prematurely. Think about being alone and how you would manage emotionally and socially. Will you move forward in your own living and loving? How will you survive the tragedy of your loss? Do you have friends and family nearby?

The tragedy of Love is that it is the partner of Death. The gift of life is going after what you want, now, not despite that inevitable happening, but because of it. One could say that love is foreplay for death.

Suggestions:

1. Read the next page alone, and then do the exercise.

2. Later, read to each other what you have written and talk about what losing your partner means to you.

3. Discuss responses to planning for eventual loss.

4. Don't explode, don't cave in, and don't leave. Just quiet yourself. This is only preliminary practice.

5. When you have finished, discuss what it was like to talk about practicing loss.

Practicing Loss

1. Bring together your thoughts about your partner and what losing him or her means to you. Write or consider that, now.

2. Write your partner's epitaph: a few words for the gravestone that express your experience of him or her.

3. Write a short note to your (live) partner. Include your appreciations, resentments, and regrets (in that order) about your history together.

4. Discuss whether you want to change anything about your relationship, and how you will plan for that.

Notes

Closing Comments

Sacred pleasure, the spiritual aspect of connecting with your beloved through erotic sex, is deliberately not addressed in this handbook. Sacred sexuality is a growing process of loving yourself, your partner, and your higher connection. This union leads you to the *sacred* meaning of erotic intimacy. It is an experience of a well-lived life.

Many, if not all, intimate moments feel sacred. Words are neither necessary nor relevant. Connecting to a higher power, and through that higher power connecting with your beloved, is a sacred act. And, connecting erotically to your beloved, and through that intimate erotic connection finding a higher power, is an equally blessed event. Couples say this reaches them through silences, mutual love for work, projects, music, art, nature, and/or the experience of having been together through great loss.

Finding a way to unite your higher self with your life-partner's higher self can and does happen through connecting physically. Tantra, as described in *The Art of Sexual Ecstasy* by Margo Anand (see Suggested Readings, p. 103), is an ancient Eastern science of spirituality expressed physically. Tantric sex encourages you toward sacred, blissful moments together and is worth exploring after you have developed the maturity and integrity to risk intense erotic energy together.

May the rest of your journey proceed with integrity, love, laughter, and relationship as a guide to glorious living.

Notes

Appendix

Toning Your Orgasm Muscles

Toning the orgasm muscles enhances orgasms for men and women. Dr. Arnold Kegel in 1940 prescribed these exercises to strengthen the puboccoxygeal (PC) muscles (the ones that help you hold urine). Not only did patients report better urinary control, they said their orgasms got stronger or took place for the first time!

Men who exercise their PC muscles often report stronger orgasms, increased ability to maintain erections, and increased ability both to delay and trigger ejaculation. PC exercises can be practiced anywhere at almost any time (except while driving or operating equipment that requires your full attention).

To identify your PC muscles: Imagine sitting on the toilet with your knees spread comfortably apart. Release and stop an imaginary flow of urine. The PC muscles are the only muscles able to stop urine flow in this position. When you recognize your PC muscles, you can exercise them in any position, unobserved: prone, sitting, standing, or walking. The only giveaway is the look on your face if you trigger an orgasm!

Like any other muscle, the PCs get painfully sore with too much exercise. Your goal is not to overexercise but rather to build muscle tone *slowly*, preferably over four to six weeks. If your PC muscles get sore, cut the exercises back by at least 75% and check with your physician if soreness persists.

The exercises can be done briefly, one to six times a day, divided into no more than five minutes at a time, and no more than fifteen minutes total in a day. Beginners should start with one minute or less and build to five minutes over several weeks. Remember to stop or rest when muscles tire. This exercise is to build pleasure, not endurance.

Exercise I: Contract and relax the PC muscles rapidly (not intensely). Begin with ten or fifteen brief and gentle contractions, build to twenty-five the first week, fifty the second, seventy-five the third, until you can do about 150 at the end of a month or two. Then add Exercise II.

Exercise II: Contract the PC muscles, hold in for four to eight seconds, then relax. Begin with five contractions and gradually, slowly, build to about fifty. When you can do fifty with ease, add Exercise III.

Exercise III: Imagine a ping pong ball rests at the opening of your vagina (anus, for males). Tighten your PC muscles as if to suck the ball slowly and deeply into the opening. Begin with about five strong "pulls" and build to fifty.

Exercising the PC muscles is particularly important for women over 35 and of any age who have given birth. Men lose PC muscle tone, too, with age. PC exercises can help your orgasm muscles regain healthy tone. After you build tone by daily practice, develop a maintenance schedule of three times a week depending on your age and health.

Suggested Readings and References

Anand, Margo. (1989). *The Art of Sexual Ecstasy: The Path of Sacred Sexuality for Western Lovers*. Los Angeles: Jeremy P. Tarcher, Inc.

Barbach, Lonnie. (1984). *For Each Other: Sharing Sexual Intimacy*. NY: New American Library.

Butler, Robert M., & Lewis, Myrna I. (1993). *Love and Sex after 60*. NY: Ballantine.

Dodson, Betty. (1987). *Sex for One: The Joy of Selfloving*. NY: Harmony Books.

Friedan, Betty. (1993). *The Fountain of Age*. NY: Simon and Schuster.

Gordon, Sol. (1990). *Why Love Is Not Enough*. Holbrook, MA: Adams Media.

Gottman, John. (1995). *Why Marriages Succeed or Fail*. NY: Simon & Schuster.

Goulding, Mary M. (1996). *A Time to Say Good-Bye: Moving Beyond Loss*. Watsonville, CA: Papier-Mache.

Hendrix, Harville. (1990). *Getting the Love You Want: A Guide for Couples*. NY: Perennial Library.

Ladas, Alice, Whipple, Beverly, & Perry, John. (1983). *The G Spot*. NY: Dell.

Love, Pat, & Robinson, Jo. (1994). *Hot Monogamy*. NY: Dutton.

Malone, Thomas P., & Malone, Patrick T. (1987). *The Art of Intimacy*. NY: Prentiss Hall.

Malone, Patrick T., & Malone, Thomas P. (1992). *The Windows of Experience*. NY: Simon & Schuster.

Morganthaler, John, & Joy, Dan. (1994). *Better Sex Through Chemistry*. Petaluma, CA: Smart Publications.

Napier, Augustus. (1988). *The Fragile Bond: In Search of an Equal, Intimate, and Enduring Marriage*. NY: Harper & Row.

Schnarch, David. (1997). *Passionate Marriage: Sex, Love, and Intimacy in Emotionally Committed Relationships*. NY: W. W. Norton.

Schwartz, Pepper. (1998). *Great Sex Weekend: A 48 hour Guide to Rekindling Sparks for Bold, Busy, or Bored Lovers*. NY: Putnam.

Tieffer, Leonore. (1995). *Sex Is Not A Natural Act & Other Essays*. Boulder: Westview.

Zilbergeld, Bernie. (1992). *The New Male Sexuality*. NY: Bantam.

Community Resources

American Academy of Psychotherapists
P.O. Box 1611
New Bern, NC 28563

    Phone: 919-634-3066Fax: 919-634-3067
    E-mail: aapoffice@aol.com

American Association of Marriage and Family Therapists
(AAMFT)
1133 15th Street NW #300
Washington, DC 20005-2710

    Phone: 202-452-0109Fax: 202-223-2329
    E-mail: www.aamft.org

American Association of Sex Educators, Counselors, and Therapists
(AASECT)
P.O. Box 238
Mount Vernon, IA 52314

    Phone: 319-895-8407Fax: 319-895-6203

The Society for the Scientific Study of Sexuality (SSSS)
P.O. Box 208
Mount Vernon, IA 52314

    Phone: 319-895-8407Fax: 319-895-6203

Sexuality Information and Education Council of the U.S. (SIECUS)
University of Pennsylvania, Graduate School of Education
3700 Walnut Street
Philadelphia, PA 19104-6216

Web access: http://www.siecus.org

Your State Psychological Association (Blue Pages in your telephone book).

State Licensure Board (Psychologists, Psychiatrists, Social Workers, Nurses, Licensed Professional Counselors, Marriage & Family Therapists).

National organizations such as these are devoted to mental and relational health, not cost containment. They can refer you to qualified couples/sex therapists in your area, should you want consultation. Please be certain that any therapist you consider has credentials from your state licensure board. Credentials from AAMFT and/or certification as a sex therapist or counselor from AASECT will indicate expertise over and above a license to practice.

Evaluation

Journey Toward Intimacy for Partner #1

Male____   Female____   Age____

Length of partnership_____

1. Please indicate your purposes in using this workbook (check all that apply):

   ____ A. To help me explore personal questions or concerns.
   ____ B. To find deeper relatedness with my partner.
   ____ C. To satisfy my curiosity.
   ____ D. Because my teacher/friend/spouse/therapist recommended it (circle all that apply).
   ____ E. To update my knowledge for marriage, work, school, career (circle all that apply).
   ____ F. Other:

2. Was the workbook personally beneficial?

   ____ A. Not at all, a waste of time and money.
   ____ B. Slightly, I got a little bit but not much.
   ____ C. Moderately, it was good in some places.
   ____ D. Very much, I got a lot from doing it.
   ____ E. Greatly, I had a transformative experience.

3. Did you complete all of the exercises, including discussions?
   ☐ Yes   ☐ No

4. Did you talk about what it was like to discuss each topic after each exercise?   □ Yes   □ No

5. Which exercises were most valuable for you? How?

6. Which exercises were least valuable for you? How?

7. What changes would you suggest?

8. Are you interested in other sexuality workbooks?

　____ A. Single Women's or Men's (circle one)
　____ B. Over 65
　____ C. Gay or Lesbian
　____ D. Physical disabilities or medical problems

Other comments?

Thank you for taking the time to give feedback, your response to this survey will help ongoing research.

Please return this form to:
Couples Enrichment Institute
P.O. Box 420114
Atlanta, GA 30342-0114

Evaluation

Journey Toward Intimacy for Partner #2

Male____   Female____   Age____

Length of partnership____

1. Please indicate your purpose(s) in using this workbook (check all that apply):

   ____ A. To help me explore personal questions or concerns.
   ____ B. To find deeper relatedness with my partner.
   ____ C. To satisfy my curiosity.
   ____ D. Because my teacher/friend/spouse/therapist recommended it (circle all that apply).
   ____ E. To update my knowledge for marriage, work, school, career (circle all that apply).
   ____ F. Other:

2. Was the workbook personally beneficial?

   ____ A. Not at all, a waste of time and money.
   ____ B. Slightly, I got a little bit but not much.
   ____ C. Moderately, it was good in some places.
   ____ D. Very much, I got a lot from doing it.
   ____ E. Greatly, I had a transformative experience.

3. Did you complete all of the exercises, including discussions?
   ☐ Yes   ☐ No

4. Did you talk about what it was like to discuss each topic after each exercise?   ☐ Yes ☐ No

5. Which exercises were most valuable for you? How?

6. Which exercises were least valuable for you? How?

7. What changes would you suggest?

8. Are you interested in other sexuality workbooks?

    ____ A. Single Women's or Men's (circle one)
    ____ B. Over 65
    ____ C. Gay or Lesbian
    ____ D. Physical disabilities or medical problems

Other comments?

Thank you for taking the time to give feedback: your response to this survey contributes to ongoing research.

Please return this form to:
Couples Enrichment Institute
P.O. Box 420114
Atlanta, GA 30342-0114

About the Author

Jeanne Slotin Shaw, Ph.D., is a grandmother, AASECT Certified Sex Therapist in practice since 1976, Clinical Director of the Couples Enrichment Institute, and clinical psychologist in private practice in Atlanta, Georgia. She has lectured and led workshops for therapists and others in the U. S. and abroad for two decades.

Author of dozens of professional articles and four handbooks, she is presently working on a book about sexual potential and aging.

She is the creator of the **Journey Toward Intimacy** Retreat for Couples weekend and a regular presenter at a variety of professional organizations, including the American Academy of Psychotherapists, American Association of Sex Educators, Counselors, and Therapists, the Society for the Scientific Study of Sex, the Society for Sex Therapy and Research, the Georgia Psychological Association, and a variety of religious, university, and medical groups.

Journey Toward Intimacy Workshops

Many of the exercises in this handbook are used in the **Journey Toward Intimacy: A Retreat for Couples** weekend workshop. The workshop meets for two days in a quiet setting near Atlanta, Georgia, and other locations.

The format includes mini-lectures, verbal and written exercises between partners, group discussion, and time alone. Like the handbook, the workshop's purpose is to encourage a sexual perspective based on self-respect, integrity, and maturity between life partners.

Our unique program helps couples, including sexual abuse survivors and their partners, to move themselves forward at their own pace with respect and awareness.

For information about sponsoring a Retreat for Couples for your organization, please contact:

The Couples Enrichment Institute
P.O. Box 420114
Atlanta, GA 30342-0114

or

www.mindspring.com/~forcouples/retreat.html

Don't Explode
Don't Cave In
Don't Leave

Quiet Yourself

Couples Enrichment Institute
P. O. Box 420114, Atlanta, GA 30342-0114

ORDER FORM

Fax orders: (404) 255-7439

Online orders: forcouples@mindspring.com

Postal orders: CEI Publications
P.O. Box 420114
Atlanta, GA 30342-0114, USA

Qty	*Journey Toward Intimacy*	Unit	Total
	A Handbook for Couples	$12.99	
	A Handbook for Lesbian Couples	$12.99	
	A Handbook for Gay Couples	$12.99	
	A Handbook for Singles	$12.99	
Please add $1.75 shipping for first book and $.50 for each book thereafter			
Total			

Payment enclosed:

☐ Check (amount in U.S. dollars): $ _____

☐ _____ ____/____
       VISA or Mastercard Number   Expiration

Signature: _____

Print Name: _____

Shipping address: _____
                          Street   Apt. No.

_____
City   State   Zip

I understand I may return any unused, resalable books for a complete refund.

ORDER FORM

Fax orders: (404) 255-7439

Online orders: forcouples@mindspring.com

Postal orders: CEI Publications
P.O. Box 420114
Atlanta, GA 30342-0114, USA

Qty	*Journey Toward Intimacy*	Unit	Total
	A Handbook for Couples	$12.99	
	A Handbook for Lesbian Couples	$12.99	
	A Handbook for Gay Couples	$12.99	
	A Handbook for Singles	$12.99	
Please add $1.75 shipping for first book and $.50 for each book thereafter			
Total			

Payment enclosed:

☐ Check (amount in U.S. dollars): $ _____

☐ _____   ____/____
　　VISA or Mastercard Number　　　　Expiration

Signature: _____

Print Name: _____

Shipping address: _____
　　　　　　　Street　　　　　　　　　　　　　Apt. No.

_____
City　　　　　　　　　　　　　　　State　　　　Zip

I understand I may return any unused, resalable books for a complete refund.